Sully the Therapy Dog

Ryan T. Witt

ISBN: 9798448642494

This book is dedicated to my wonderful family. To my Mom, Dad, Sister, and Wife. Thank you for your love and belief in my ever-changing aspirations.

– Ryan

Hi, my name is Sully!

I am a Golden Retriever.

I am one year old.

My birthday is in December.

When is your birthday?

I live at home with my mommy and daddy.

I love to play with my toys!

I have a big brother named Tucker.

I have a little sister named Muffin.

Do you have any siblings?

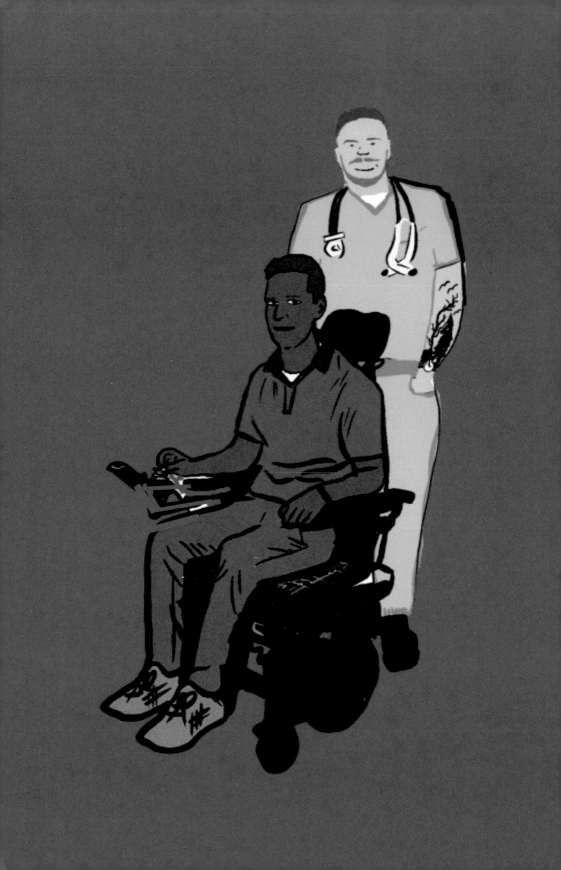

My dad is going to be an Occupational Therapist.

They help people keep doing the things they love to do.

Dad wants me to work with him.

What job could I do?

I could visit people in the hospital.

I could make people smile when they are having a bad day.

I could make some new friends!

Would you be my friend?

I could work at a school.

I would visit lots of kids.

The students could read me a story.

Have you seen a doggy at school?

I could visit the nursing home.

I think they would give me treats.

The people are older, but they pet me so sweet.

Do you think I'd like the nursing home?

Where do you think Sully will work?

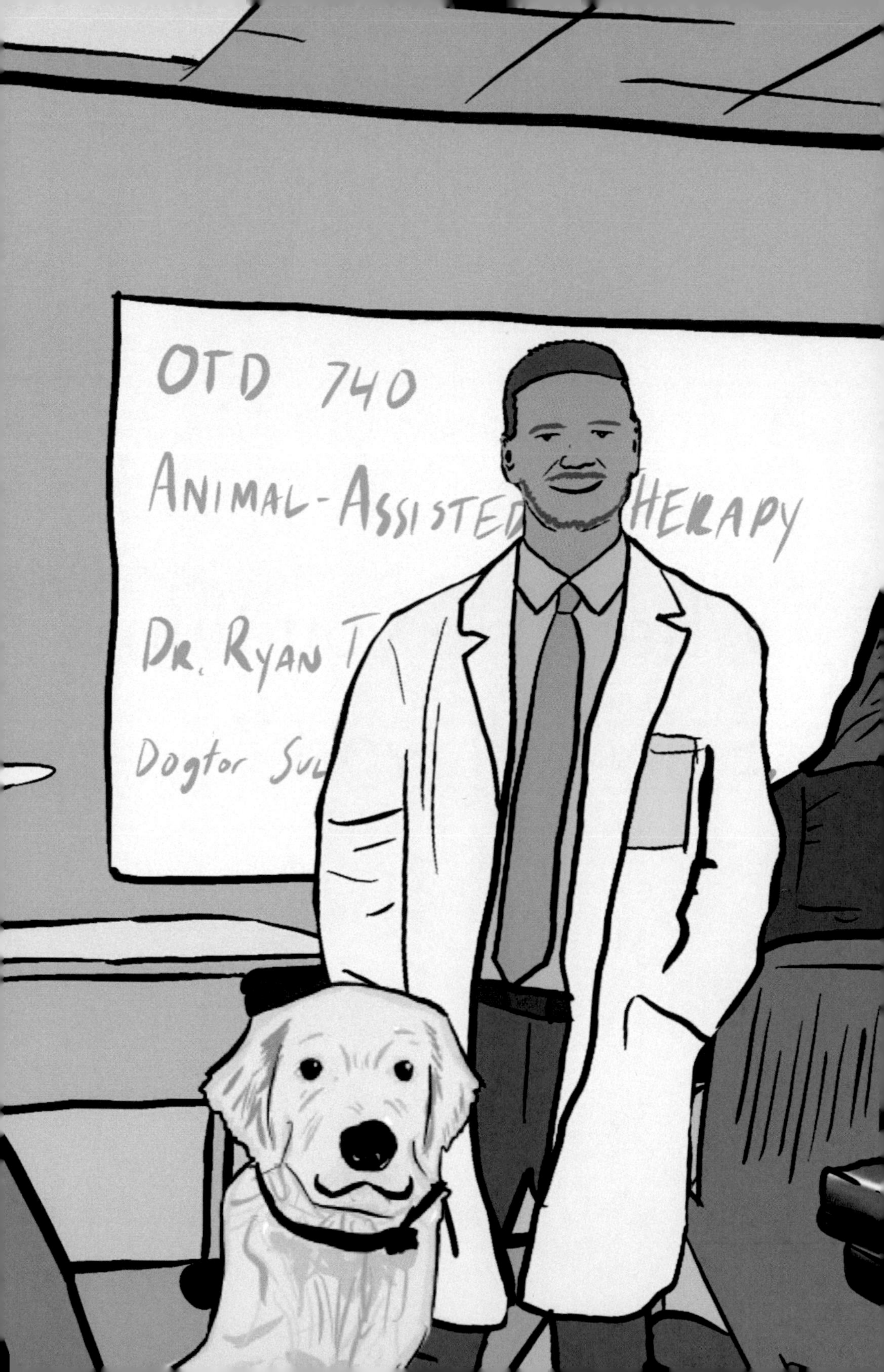

OTD 740
ANIMAL-ASSISTED
HERAPY
DR. RYAN
Dogtor

I am going to a special school with my daddy.

He is going to teach future therapists about my job.

I am going to show them how I train.

We will visit the elementary school, the hospital, and the nursing home.

I will be sleepy when I get home!

I am Sully,
the therapy dog.

The Authors

Ryan T. Witt is an Occupational Therapy student at Huntington University in Fort Wayne, IN. Currently, he is working on creating the doctoral program's first animal-assisted therapy course available for students that he will teach upon graduation in May of 2023.

Sully is a one-year-old English Cream Golden Retriever. He has earned his AKC Trick Dog Novice title and will be evaluated for his official Therapy Dog title at the end of May 2022.

For additional information follow Sully's Instagram account- @james.phillip.sullivan